14 Days Crash Course to Financial Confidence

14 Days Crash Course to Financial Confidence

© [08/11/2024] [Maxwell W. Wilson]

Independently Published

Cover design by Maxwell W. Wilson

ISBN: [9798345767795]

Disclaimer : *This book is for informational purposes only. While every effort has been made to ensure the accuracy and completeness of the information contained herein, the author and publisher assume no responsibility for errors, inaccuracies, omissions, or any outcomes resulting from the use of this information. The content is provided on an "as-is" basis and does not constitute professional or technical advice. Readers are encouraged to consult official sources and professionals for specific guidance.*

Trademarks : *All brand names and product names used in this book are trademarks, registered trademarks, or trade names of their respective holders. The use of trademarks is for reference only and does not imply any affiliation with or endorsement by the trademark holders.*

For permissions, media inquiries, or publishing opportunities, please contact the author at: sspider1012@gmail.com

"Wealth consists not in having great possessions, but in having few wants."

Epictetus

Preface

This book is for Individuals who want a simple, effective approach to managing money. It's a two-week crash course, designed to strip away the noise and leave you with a clear path to financial confidence.

I wrote this book because, like many salaried professionals, I used to feel overwhelmed by financial advice that seemed more complicated than helpful. It took years of trial and error, along with a commitment to adopting minimalist principles, to realize that financial success doesn't have to be complex. In fact, the simpler you make your financial plan, the more likely you are to stick to it and see lasting results.

Over the next two weeks, you'll discover that managing money isn't about earning the highest salary or mastering every investment strategy—it's about making consistent, intentional choices with what you have. You'll learn how to reduce financial clutter, prioritize what matters, and adopt practical habits that can work for anyone on a salary. Each day focuses on one practical step, from budgeting essentials to debt management, saving strategies, and making your money work harder for you.

Contents

Introduction: The 2-Week Crash Course to Financial Minimalism

Welcome to the *2 Week Crash Course* that will revolutionize the way you handle money. Yes, I know "revolutionize" is a big promise—right up there with life-changing toasters and miracle weight-loss teas. But seriously, this course has one goal: to simplify your financial life in just 14 days, using tried-and-true principles of minimalist money management.

So, what exactly are we getting into here? Minimalism, as a lifestyle, has gained serious traction in recent years. You've probably heard about people who live in tiny houses or happily own just one pair of jeans. That's not quite what we're doing with your finances, but the idea is the same: decluttering and simplifying. We're ditching the financial equivalent of that closet full of outdated clothes that's been dragging you down.

This book won't give you an overly complicated, jargon-filled financial masterclass. Instead, it's designed to spoon-feed you (hey, no shame in that) practical, actionable advice, day by day, over the next two weeks. So let's jump in, coffee in hand, and start laying the groundwork for a stress-free, wealth-building journey.

Why Minimalist Money Management?

Before we dive into the nuts and bolts, let's get one thing straight: the minimalist approach to finances isn't about being cheap or denying yourself life's pleasures. It's about intentionality. It's about realizing that every dollar you spend is a little chunk of your freedom, and that chunk is either working for you or against you.

Here's the harsh truth: most of us have way more financial "stuff" than we need—multiple credit cards we don't use, subscriptions to things we don't remember signing up for, and random investments our cousin convinced us were a good idea at last year's Thanksgiving. If our financial lives were houses, they'd be full of clutter. Minimalism cuts through that.

Now, minimalist money management comes with two critical benefits: *simplicity* and *focus*. We'll strip down your finances to the essentials, make your money management process so straightforward that even your dog could probably follow along (although I still don't recommend handing over your savings account password to Fido), and give you a roadmap to achieving financial freedom faster. Imagine what it feels like to have clarity, to know where every dollar is going and to be able to use your resources for what truly matters. That's what we're aiming for.

What to Expect Over the Next Two Weeks

Let me break down what we'll cover over the next two weeks. Think of it like a Netflix binge for your financial life, except (hopefully) more enlightening and far less guilt-inducing.

- **Week 1**: We'll lay the foundation by understanding your current financial picture, identifying what's essential, and creating a streamlined budget. By Day 7, you'll have a clear, minimalistic snapshot of your finances.

- **Week 2**: We shift gears to building wealth and maintaining it with the same minimalist principles. From simplifying your investments to automating your finances, you'll learn how to build and sustain your newfound wealth.

2

If you follow this plan step by step—and you promise to be honest with yourself about your finances (we all have our guilty pleasures, but this is a judgment-free zone)—you'll come out of these two weeks with a clear, actionable plan and the confidence to handle your money like a pro.

Setting the Tone: A Reality Check

Okay, so let's address the big elephant in the room: personal finance can be boring. I mean, unless spreadsheets get your heart racing, you probably don't spend your weekends thinking about how to maximize your Roth IRA contributions. But here's the thing: *boring* isn't necessarily bad. Sometimes, the best strategies in life are painfully simple, and when it comes to money, simple is sexy.

But to sweeten the deal, I'll try to keep things as light as possible, adding a joke here and there. (Although fair warning: I make no promises about the quality of said jokes.) We'll laugh at some common financial pitfalls—like that time you bought an artisanal cheese subscription you totally forgot about—and celebrate the small wins, like brewing your own coffee instead of buying yet another $6 oat milk latte.

Humor aside, this course is serious about delivering results. You're here because you want to make meaningful changes, and by the end of these 14 days, you will. Whether your goal is to pay off debt, save for a down payment, or retire before age 80, this course gives you the blueprint to get there.

How to Use This Crash Course

Each day's content is designed to be manageable—think 20 to 30 minutes of focused work. By taking small but consistent actions, you'll create lasting habits. And remember, financial freedom is a marathon, not a sprint. Unless you win the lottery, and then, well... that's a different book altogether.

You might be tempted to jump around, but trust the process. Each chapter builds on the one before, so skipping ahead would be like fast-forwarding through a mystery movie and missing all the clues. You'll get to the good stuff, I promise.

Grab a pen, a notebook, and maybe a calming herbal tea (or wine, no judgment). Let's simplify, declutter, and make those financial dreams a reality. See you in Chapter One!

Key Principles of Minimalist Money Management

Alright, let's get down to the bedrock of minimalist money management. Before we dive headlong into budgets and savings plans, we need to establish some core principles. Think of these as your financial North Star—guiding you, grounding you, and hopefully preventing you from panic-buying a robotic vacuum cleaner you never knew you needed.

1. Less Is More

At the heart of minimalist money management is a simple yet powerful concept: *less is more*. And no, this doesn't mean depriving yourself of joy or living like a monk (unless that's your thing, in which case, more power to you). It's about clearing out the financial clutter to make space for what truly matters. Here's how this translates into practical steps:

- **Fewer Accounts, More Simplicity**: Instead of juggling five different credit cards and a rainbow of bank accounts, consider consolidating. Choose a primary checking

4

account, a high-yield savings account, and a straightforward credit card that rewards you for the spending you already do.

- **Quality Over Quantity**: When making purchases, focus on quality rather than quantity. Would you rather have five pairs of cheap shoes that wear out in a year or one durable, high-quality pair that lasts for five years? Investing in quality items saves you money in the long run.

If your closet still holds that impulse buy from a late-night infomercial, remember: financial minimalism means fewer regrets... and maybe fewer pairs of bedazzled slippers.

2. Intentionality Is Everything

Minimalism isn't just about reducing—it's about being intentional. Every financial decision you make should serve a purpose. It's about putting your dollars to work in ways that align with your values and long-term goals. Think of each dollar as a little employee. Where would you rather they work: building your future wealth or funding some random corporation's next yacht party?

To be more intentional:

- **Know Your Values**: What are the things that bring you true joy? Travel? Time with family? Pursuing your passion project? When you know your core values, you can make financial decisions that reflect them.

- **Align Spending with Goals**: If your dream is to take a sabbatical and travel, then every $100 you don't spend on dining out is another $100 toward that dream.

Budgeting becomes less about restriction and more about prioritizing what you love.

3. Automation Is Your Friend

We're not about making you work harder, but *smarter*. Automation takes the guesswork out of money management and reduces the temptation to overspend. Once you've determined your budget, automate as many processes as you can:

- **Savings**: Set up automatic transfers from your checking to your savings account as soon as you get paid. Think of this as paying your future self first.

- **Investments**: Contribute to your retirement and investment accounts automatically. The beauty of automation is that your money grows in the background, without you lifting a finger.

- **Bills**: Automate recurring bills like rent, utilities, and insurance. This reduces stress and ensures you never miss a payment.

Quick Tip: Remember that automation doesn't mean you can set and forget your finances forever. A monthly financial check-in is essential to make sure everything's on track.

4. Embrace the Power of the 80/20 Rule

Ever heard of the Pareto Principle? It states that roughly 80% of outcomes come from 20% of efforts. In the world of finance, this translates to focusing on the most impactful strategies. Instead of getting caught up in penny-pinching every little expense, identify the few big financial levers you can pull to make a real difference.

- **Focus on Major Wins**: Negotiating a lower interest rate on your mortgage or cutting your car insurance bill by 15% has a bigger impact than obsessing over the cost of your daily coffee.

- **Simplify Investments**: Instead of trying to pick the next winning stock, consider low-fee index funds. They're simple, cost-effective, and proven to perform well over the long term.

5. Value Financial Freedom Over Status

Minimalist money management is about prioritizing financial freedom over the illusion of wealth. It's easy to get sucked into the status game—wanting to upgrade to a luxury car because your neighbor did or buying the latest gadget to keep up with trends. But remember, true wealth is the ability to live life on your terms, not having flashy things that keep you in a cycle of work and debt.

Ask yourself: Would you rather have a shiny new car with a five-year loan or the freedom to quit your job and travel for six months? Sometimes, the greatest luxuries aren't things at all.

Applying These Principles to Your Life

Now that we've covered the basics, here's how to start applying these principles:

1. **Audit Your Financial Life**: Where can you declutter? Are there old, unused accounts or subscriptions that you can cancel?

2. **Identify Your Core Values**: Sit down with a journal and write out the things that are most important to you. Are your financial habits supporting these values?

3. **Automate and Simplify**: Take a day to automate your savings and investments. Set calendar reminders for a monthly financial check-in.

Minimalist money management isn't about perfection. It's about progress. Even the smallest steps can lead to significant changes. You'll have setbacks, and that's okay. Remember, the goal is a simpler, more intentional approach to your money—an approach that gives you the freedom to live your best life.

Day 1: Understanding Financial Minimalism and Your Money Mindset

Congratulations, you've officially embarked on your minimalist money management journey! Today is all about grasping the core principles of financial minimalism and getting real with your money mindset. Don't worry, there's no need to lie on a therapy couch or confront childhood traumas (unless you're into that). Instead, we'll be tackling how your relationship with money influences your financial choices—and how to shift your thinking for good.

The Core Principles of Financial Minimalism

First off, let's explore what "financial minimalism" really means. It's more than just cutting costs and living on instant ramen (unless you're truly a noodle enthusiast). Financial minimalism is a holistic, intentional approach to managing money. Here's what we're talking about:

1. **Intentional Spending Over Mindless Consumption**

   o   Every dollar you spend should have a purpose, whether it's saving for a dream vacation, buying organic avocados (because who doesn't love a good guacamole?), or investing in your future. Financial minimalism is about making choices that align with your values rather than giving in to consumerism's shiny allure.

2. **Simplicity in Financial Management**

   o Simplify, simplify, simplify! If you've ever felt overwhelmed by your finances, this is your permission to cut out the noise. Fewer accounts, fewer credit cards, and a simplified budget reduce financial stress and free up your mental space.

3. **Focusing on Long-Term Fulfillment Over Short-Term Gratification**

   o The joy of a new gadget or a shopping spree fades quickly, but the satisfaction of financial security lasts. Minimalist money management emphasizes delayed gratification and investing in experiences or assets that yield long-term benefits.

Practical Example: Imagine being at a checkout line and seeing a last-minute "deal" on a cute but impractical kitchen gadget. Financial minimalism asks you to pause and ask: Does this align with my financial goals? More often than not, you'll find the answer is a resounding "no."

Shifting Your Mindset: From Consumerism to Intentional Living

Ah, the infamous money mindset. It's the silent puppet master pulling the strings on how you earn, save, and spend. Today, we're going to uncover those invisible strings and start making some changes.

Step 1: Uncovering Your Current Money Mindset

First things first, let's take a look at your existing beliefs about money. These are often shaped by upbringing, culture, and life experiences. For example:

- Did your parents teach you to save every penny, or did they live paycheck to paycheck?

- Do you view money as a scarce resource to hoard, or a tool to improve your life and the lives of others?

Take a moment to reflect. Jot down some of your core beliefs about money. Don't overthink it; just let the ideas flow. Maybe you've been telling yourself, "I'll never be good with money," or "I need to have the latest tech to be happy." Identifying these beliefs is crucial because they affect how you handle your finances.

If your money mindset were a character in a movie, would it be a paranoid conspiracy theorist, a carefree spender on a shopping spree, or a frugal wizard guarding a pile of gold? (It's okay; we all have a mix of characters up there.)

Step 2: Understanding the Trap of Consumerism

Consumerism is everywhere. It's in the ads that promise happiness with a new purchase, the sales that make you feel like you're losing money by *not* buying something, and the subtle peer pressure to keep up with your friends' seemingly glamorous lives.

But here's the truth: *More stuff rarely equals more happiness.* Studies consistently show that experiences and financial security bring far greater joy than material goods. Financial minimalism asks you to flip the script: instead of spending to impress others, spend to invest in yourself and your future.

Quick Thought Experiment: Imagine you suddenly inherited $1 million. What's the first thing you'd do? If your mind races to luxury cars or designer clothes, don't worry. We've been trained to think this way. But now, imagine using that money to pay off debts, invest for the future, or even buy back your time by working fewer hours. Feels different, doesn't it?

Step 3: Rewriting Your Money Story

Here's where things get exciting: it's time to change the narrative. Just because you've always believed one thing about money doesn't mean it has to stay that way. Rewriting your money story means adopting a mindset that promotes financial health and freedom.

- **Affirmations**: Replace negative beliefs with empowering ones. Instead of "I'm bad with money," try "I'm learning to manage my money wisely and confidently."

- **Visualizations**: Spend a few minutes each day visualizing your financial goals. Picture yourself debt-free, traveling the world, or retiring early. This helps reprogram your subconscious to believe in your financial success.

- **Positive Money Habits**: Start small. If you've never budgeted before, create a simple one. If you tend to splurge, implement a 24-hour rule: wait a day before making any non-essential purchase.

Pro Tip: Treat your finances like a garden. It takes time to grow and requires regular attention. Weed out bad habits, plant seeds of investment, and watch your wealth flourish.

Your Day 1 Action Plan

1. **Reflect on Your Money Mindset**: Take 10 minutes to write down your current beliefs about money. Be honest—this is for your eyes only.

2. **Identify One Habit to Change**: Maybe it's resisting impulse buys, or maybe it's checking your bank balance regularly. Pick one habit and commit to changing it.

3. **Practice Gratitude**: Financial minimalism isn't just about having less; it's about appreciating what you already have. List three things you're grateful for that don't involve spending money.

By the end of today, you'll have a better understanding of how your mindset impacts your money habits. You'll be ready to shift from a consumer-driven lifestyle to one that prioritizes intentionality and long-term happiness. And hey, if you're still tempted by that robotic vacuum, remember: less is more... unless it also makes coffee, in which case, all bets are off.

Day 2: Calculating Your Baseline and Understanding Your Expenses

Welcome to Day 2! Yesterday, we delved into the mindset shifts necessary for financial minimalism, and now it's time to get into the nitty-gritty: understanding your expenses. No, this isn't the most glamorous part of our crash course, but trust me, it's essential. After today, you'll have a clear picture of your financial baseline, which is the foundation of our minimalist money plan. Ready to roll up your sleeves? Let's do this.

Analyzing What You Truly Need to Live

First things first: what's your financial baseline? This is the minimum amount of money you need each month to cover your non-negotiable living expenses. Think of it as your financial survival number—the budget that keeps a roof over your head, the lights on, and food in your belly, minus any extras or splurges.

Step 1: Identify Your Essentials Let's break down what qualifies as a true need. Basic living expenses generally include:

- **Housing**: Rent or mortgage payments, property taxes, and basic utilities like electricity, water, and gas.

- **Groceries**: Not takeout or those fancy $7 cold-pressed juices, but the actual cost of food that sustains you.

- **Transportation**: Gas, car payments, insurance, or public transportation costs. If you work remotely, adjust accordingly.

- **Healthcare**: Insurance premiums and average monthly medication costs.

- **Minimum Debt Payments**: Any loans or credit card bills that have to be paid to avoid penalties.

Now, add up these amounts. This total represents your financial baseline. If the number surprises or scares you, remember that today is about *awareness*, not judgment. This is the foundation we'll build upon.

Practical Exercise: Write down your baseline number and consider keeping it visible—stick it on your fridge, your desk, or your bathroom mirror. It's a powerful reminder of your financial reality.

If your list of "essentials" starts to include your Netflix subscription or an emergency fund for late-night sushi cravings, that's your cue to get real with yourself.

Categorizing Expenses: Needs vs. Wants

Once we know what you *need* to live, it's time to get honest about the rest. This is where financial minimalism shines: separating needs from wants. Spoiler alert: this might sting a little, especially if you love your daily gourmet coffee runs or weekly retail therapy.

Step 1: List Out Your Monthly Expenses Grab your last three months of bank and credit card statements. Seriously, go get them. We're doing this together, friend. As you review your spending, create two columns:

- **Needs**: These are your essentials, as we discussed. They're the costs you can't live without.

- **Wants**: These are the discretionary expenses. They're fun, enjoyable, and add spice to life, but they're not necessary for survival.

Examples of Wants:

- Streaming services (because, let's be real, you probably don't need six of them)

- Dining out and takeout

- Gym memberships or fitness classes (especially if you have free alternatives)

- Shopping for clothes, gadgets, or home décor

Reality Check: This exercise isn't about shaming yourself into ascetic living. It's about recognizing what truly adds value to your life versus what drains your wallet with little return. Maybe that yoga studio membership brings you peace and joy, while those forgotten magazine subscriptions are dead weight. The goal here is to prioritize consciously.

Quick and Effective Methods to Track Spending

Okay, you've categorized your spending, but how do you make sure you're sticking to your plan going forward? Enter the world of expense tracking! (I promise, it's less boring than it sounds.)

1. The "Old-School" Method: Manual Tracking

If you prefer hands-on control, a simple spreadsheet might be your best friend. Create columns for:

- Date
- Expense Category (e.g., Groceries, Transportation, Entertainment)
- Amount

Update this regularly—daily or weekly—so you always know where your money is going. If you're a paper-and-pen kind of person, a financial journal can be just as effective.

Pro Tip: Dedicate 10 minutes every Sunday to review your spending. Light a candle, brew some tea, or make it a ritual to keep things zen.

2. The "Set-It-and-Forget-It" Method: Budgeting Apps

Not a fan of manual tracking? Budgeting apps can automate the process. Popular options like Mint, YNAB (You Need A Budget), or PocketGuard sync with your bank accounts, categorizing expenses for you. They also send helpful alerts to keep you within budget.

App Suggestions:

- **Mint**: Great for beginners. It tracks spending, creates budgets, and even gives you a credit score update.

- **YNAB**: A favorite for those who want to be more hands-on with their budget. It's all about giving every dollar a job.

- **PocketGuard**: Keeps things simple by showing you how much money you have available to spend after your bills and savings goals.

3. The Envelope Method

Feeling nostalgic or want a visual, tactile way to control spending? Try the envelope method: withdraw cash for discretionary spending categories (like dining out, entertainment, etc.) and place the cash in separate envelopes. When the envelope is empty, that's it—no more spending in that category until next month. It's a great way to curb overspending if you struggle with credit card discipline.

Your Day 2 Action Plan

1. **Calculate Your Baseline**: Add up your essential expenses and write down the total. This number is your financial foundation.

2. **Categorize Your Expenses**: Go through your last three months of statements and split your spending into "Needs" and "Wants." Be honest with yourself.

3. **Choose Your Tracking Method**: Pick one of the tracking strategies above and commit to it for the next two weeks. Automation? Spreadsheets? Envelopes? Whatever works best for you.

By the end of today, you'll not only know your financial baseline but also have a clear understanding of where your money goes. This knowledge is powerful—it gives you control and sets the stage for purposeful financial decisions. Plus, remember: every small step you take now is a giant leap toward financial freedom.

Feeling a bit more in control already? Good! Let's keep this momentum going. Tomorrow, we'll start tackling how to create a minimalist, stress-free budget. See you then!

Day 3: Setting Financial Goals with Minimalist Intentions

You've made it to Day 3! By now, you understand your financial baseline and have a clearer idea of where your money goes. Today, we're taking a more inspiring turn: setting financial goals that align with your minimalist lifestyle and values. Think of this as building your financial roadmap, with a destination that truly matters to *you*.

Defining Short-Term, Medium-Term, and Long-Term Goals

First up, let's categorize our dreams. Breaking down financial goals into manageable timeframes makes them more achievable and keeps you motivated. But remember: minimalist money management isn't just about acquiring wealth for wealth's sake. It's about creating a life that feels rich in experience, security, and freedom.

1. Short-Term Goals (0-1 Year)

These are the quick wins, the goals you can tackle in the next year or less. Short-term goals should feel tangible and achievable without completely upending your life. They're like the first rung on a ladder, helping you climb toward bigger financial dreams.

Examples of Short-Term Goals:

- Building an emergency fund (aim for $1,000 to start, then gradually increase)

- Paying off a small debt, like a high-interest credit card balance

- Creating a realistic monthly budget and sticking to it

- Saving for an upcoming trip or a special occasion

Practical Tip: Prioritize these goals based on urgency. If your car needs repairs soon or you're planning a big move, those should take precedence. Use SMART criteria: Specific, Measurable, Achievable, Relevant, and Time-bound.

Treat your short-term goals like a series of fun, personal challenges. Think of it as "financial gamification." If hitting your emergency fund goal means you can finally breathe easier, that's a victory dance moment!

---

2. Medium-Term Goals (1-5 Years)

Medium-term goals require a bit more planning and discipline but are still within sight. These goals are often linked to life transitions or achievements you want to reach within the next few years.

Examples of Medium-Term Goals:

- Paying off student loans or a significant portion of other debt

- Saving for a down payment on a house (or another major purchase)

- Funding a significant life event, like a wedding or starting a family

- Advancing your career through education or a certification course

How to Approach Medium-Term Goals:

- **Consistency Is Key**: For these goals, consistency trumps everything. Automate your savings or debt payments so you never miss a contribution.

- **Create a Dedicated Savings Account**: If you're saving for a house or other major expense, consider a separate high-yield savings account to watch your money grow faster.

Quick Thought: Visualize the payoff of each goal. Imagine the relief of being debt-free or the joy of stepping into your first home. This makes saving feel more meaningful and less like a chore.

---

3. Long-Term Goals (5+ Years)

Now we're looking at the big-picture stuff. Long-term goals often focus on financial security and future-proofing your life. They can seem intimidating, but breaking them down into smaller steps helps.

Examples of Long-Term Goals:

- Saving for retirement (max out your 401(k) or IRA if possible)

- Investing in the stock market for long-term wealth growth

- Paying off your mortgage or saving for a second property

- Planning for your child's education fund

Key Strategies for Long-Term Goals:

- **Invest Wisely**: Time is your best friend when it comes to investing. Even small amounts can grow significantly over 20-30 years, thanks to compound interest.

- **Think Beyond Money**: Long-term goals can also include non-financial aspirations, like early retirement to pursue your passion or having the financial freedom to travel extensively.

Think of your long-term goals like a fine wine—better with time. Patience and discipline now mean a richer life later.

The Power of Goal Alignment with Your Values

Okay, now let's make sure your goals actually mean something to you. Financial minimalism is about aligning your money with what you genuinely value. Here's how to make sure you're on the right track:

1. **Define Your Core Values**: Grab a piece of paper and write down the three to five things that matter most to you. It could be family, health, travel, career growth, or giving back to your community. These values should shape your financial decisions.

2. **Align Your Goals with These Values**: Review your short-, medium-, and long-term goals. Do they reflect what's truly important to you? If not, adjust them. For example:

   - If health is a core value, investing in a gym membership or healthy meal services may be more important than upgrading to the latest tech.

- o   If freedom is a key value, early retirement might be worth prioritizing over a luxury lifestyle.

3. **Cut Out Goal "Noise"**: Society often pressures us to chase goals that don't align with our values—like owning a giant house or a flashy car. If these things don't genuinely fulfill you, let them go. Your goals should serve *you*, not anyone else's expectations.

Reflective Question: Ask yourself, "Will this goal bring me closer to a life that feels rich, meaningful, and fulfilling?" If the answer is yes, you're on the right track.

Your Day 3 Action Plan

1. **Write Down Your Goals**: Categorize them into short-, medium-, and long-term, and be specific about what you want to achieve.

2. **Make Each Goal SMART**: Outline how you'll measure success and the time frame for each goal.

3. **Create a Vision Board**: If you're a visual person, consider making a vision board for your financial future. It's a fun, creative way to stay inspired.

4. **Align Your Goals with Your Values**: Check that your goals reflect what's truly important to you. If not, tweak them.

Remember, setting financial goals is not about restriction; it's about liberation. You're giving yourself the gift of a purposeful, value-driven financial life. Tomorrow, we'll take this newfound focus and start building a minimalist budget to make those goals a reality.

Day 4: Creating a Minimalist Budget

Welcome to Day 4! Today, we're diving into what some might call the heart of financial minimalism: budgeting. I know, I know—budgeting can sound as appealing as getting a root canal. But hang tight, because a minimalist budget isn't about endless spreadsheets or denying yourself the joys of life. It's about crafting a plan that's simple, effective, and aligned with what you care about most.

Streamlining Your Budget with Simple Methods

The first step to financial clarity is trimming down your budget to its essentials. We're not aiming for perfection here—just simplicity and effectiveness.

1. Start with the 50/30/20 Rule (Minimalist Style)

This tried-and-true budgeting method can be easily adapted to fit a minimalist framework. Here's how it works:

- **50% Needs**: These are your essential expenses, like rent, utilities, groceries, insurance, and transportation. This category should cover the non-negotiables that keep you functional and safe.

- **30% Wants**: This is for lifestyle-related expenses, like dining out, entertainment, travel, and hobbies. Remember, minimalism doesn't mean a joyless existence; it means spending on things that bring genuine value.

- **20% Savings and Debt Repayment**: This includes retirement savings, emergency fund contributions, and paying down debt. If you're serious about building long-term financial security, treat this category as a non-negotiable commitment.

Practical Tip: If your needs take up more than 50% of your income, adjust your budget gradually. The goal isn't to squeeze your life dry but to realign your spending so you can prioritize savings and meaningful experiences.

2. The "Two-Account" Method

Another minimalist favorite is the Two-Account Method. Here's how it works:

- **Account #1: Essentials Account**: This is where you pay for rent, bills, groceries, and other needs. Automate as many payments as possible so you can set it and forget it.

- **Account #2: Discretionary Account**: Transfer your monthly "wants" and discretionary spending money here. Once it's gone, it's gone. This method helps you limit overspending without micro-managing your budget.

Bonus: The simplicity of having only two accounts can be liberating, making money management less stressful and more intuitive.

Tools for Managing Your Money Effortlessly

Who says managing money has to be a drag? In our tech-savvy world, there are plenty of apps and tools that make budgeting feel like less of a chore. Here are some minimalist-approved options:

1. Minimalist Budgeting Apps

- **YNAB (You Need A Budget)**: Ideal for those who want to give every dollar a job. YNAB encourages you to be intentional with every expense and has a cult-like following for a reason.

- **Mint**: This app connects to your bank accounts and tracks your spending automatically. It gives you a clear, up-to-date picture of where your money is going and helps you spot overspending patterns.

- **PocketGuard**: Perfect for beginners, this app shows you how much money you have left to spend after accounting for bills, goals, and savings.

Pro Tip: The key to using these tools effectively is consistency. Dedicate 5-10 minutes a week to check in with your finances. Pair it with your favorite cup of tea or make it part of your Sunday morning ritual.

2. Old-School, Pen-and-Paper Method

If digital tools aren't your thing, a simple notebook works just fine. The act of writing down your expenses can make you more conscious of your spending habits. Plus, it's a great excuse to invest in some beautiful stationery if that's something you love.

Minimalist Budget Template:

- **Income**: List all sources of income for the month.

- **Expenses**: Divide into needs, wants, and savings. Keep it simple and straightforward.

- **Review**: Check in weekly to see if you're on track.

Balancing Essential Living with Enjoyment

Minimalism isn't about deprivation. It's about being intentional, even when it comes to treating yourself. Let's talk about how to balance essential living with joy:

1. Make Room for What Matters

Maybe you love traveling, dining out, or collecting vinyl records. A minimalist budget doesn't force you to cut these out; it encourages you to spend intentionally. Allocate a portion of your budget for the things that truly make your life richer and eliminate expenses that don't serve you.

Reflective Exercise: Write down three things that bring you the most happiness. Are you allocating your budget to support these experiences or items? If not, adjust your spending to prioritize what you love.

2. Embrace the "One In, One Out" Rule

To prevent clutter—financial and otherwise—try the "One In, One Out" rule. If you buy something new, let go of an old item of similar value or utility. This helps maintain balance and keeps your spending in check.

Example: If you splurge on a new tech gadget, consider selling or donating an older one. This approach applies to physical items as well as subscription services.

3. Find Low-Cost (or No-Cost) Joys

Sometimes, the best things in life really are free—or at least cheap. Explore local parks, attend free community events, or have a DIY movie night with friends. Being mindful of your spending doesn't mean missing out on fun; it means getting creative and appreciating the simpler pleasures.

Hey, if watching cat videos online is your guilty pleasure, make sure your budget has room for a stable internet connection. Happiness matters!

Your Day 4 Action Plan

1. **Choose Your Budgeting Method**: Decide if you want to use the 50/30/20 rule, the Two-Account Method, or something else entirely. Simplicity is key.

2. **Pick a Budgeting Tool**: Download a budgeting app or grab a notebook to start tracking your expenses.

3. **Schedule a Weekly Money Date**: Spend 10 minutes reviewing your finances. Make it a habit, and feel the empowerment grow.

Budgeting, when done the minimalist way, is about creating freedom, not limitations. By streamlining your money management, you'll find more space—financially and mentally—for what truly matters.

Day 5: Cutting Financial Clutter and Unnecessary Expenses

It's Day 5, and you're on a roll! Today, we're decluttering not just our closets, but our wallets and bank accounts, too. Financial clutter may not take up physical space, but it sure can weigh heavily on your mind and drain your finances. The goal here is to simplify, optimize, and make sure every dollar works for you, not against you.

Reducing Bills and Managing Subscriptions

Let's face it—those recurring expenses can sneak up on you like a ninja. One day you're signing up for a "free trial," and the next thing you know, you're subscribed to five streaming services you barely use. Cutting these sneaky expenses is like finding hidden money in your couch cushions.

1. Audit Your Recurring Expenses

Make a list of all your subscriptions and monthly bills. This includes streaming services, gym memberships, app subscriptions, and even the small ones that seem inconsequential. You can do this manually or use an app like **Truebill** or **Trim** to help track and cancel unwanted subscriptions.

Practical Exercise: Print out your bank and credit card statements from the last three months. Highlight any recurring charges you don't fully recognize or rarely use. Ask yourself, "Does this subscription bring me real value?" If not, cancel it. Boom—instant savings.

Pro Tip: Some companies offer discounts or promotions if you attempt to cancel a subscription. Take advantage of these, but only if you genuinely value the service.

---

2. Negotiate Your Bills

Yes, you can negotiate certain bills, like your internet, cable, or even insurance premiums. It might feel uncomfortable at first, but trust me—it's worth it.

How to Negotiate:

- **Be Prepared**: Research competitor rates and have that information handy.

- **Be Polite but Firm**: Call your provider, and let them know you're considering switching to a cheaper competitor. Ask if they can match or beat the price.

- **Ask for Discounts**: Many companies offer discounts if you're a loyal customer or if you pay your bill in advance.

Example Script: "Hi, I noticed that my internet bill has gone up. I've seen offers from [Competitor] for a lower rate. I'd love to stay with you if you can match that price or provide me with a discount."

Simplifying Banking and Credit Card Accounts

A minimalist financial setup means fewer accounts to manage and less mental clutter. Simplifying your banking can help you keep better track of your money and reduce fees.

1. Consolidate Your Bank Accounts

If you have multiple checking and savings accounts at different banks, consider consolidating them. Choose a bank that offers fee-free accounts and has the features you need, like a high-yield savings account or a robust mobile app. This way, you'll have a clearer picture of your finances and fewer statements to sort through.

Practical Tip: Keep at least two accounts—a checking account for everyday transactions and a high-yield savings account for your emergency fund. Beyond that, only open accounts that have a specific purpose (like a separate account for a big savings goal).

2. Simplify Your Credit Cards

Credit cards can be both a blessing and a curse. If you have too many cards, it can become overwhelming to keep track of balances, payments, and annual fees.

Steps to Simplify Your Credit Cards:

1. **Choose One or Two Cards with the Best Benefits**: Focus on cards with no annual fees or ones that offer meaningful rewards (like cash back or travel points).

2. **Pay Off and Close Unnecessary Accounts**: If you have cards with high fees or no useful benefits, pay them off and consider closing the accounts. Just be mindful of how this might impact your credit score.

Pro Tip: Set up autopay for your credit card balances to avoid late fees, and use alerts to remind you of upcoming due dates.

Strategies for Living Below Your Means

Living below your means is the cornerstone of financial minimalism. It's about spending less than you earn and finding contentment in simplicity.

1. Adopt the "Anti-Budget" Approach

If traditional budgets make you want to run for the hills, try the anti-budget. Here's how it works:

- First, automatically save a set percentage of your income each month. Think of it as paying yourself first.

- Then, spend whatever's left guilt-free. This method encourages you to prioritize saving without tracking every dollar you spend.

Example: If you decide to save 20% of your income, set up an automatic transfer to your savings account on payday. The rest is yours to spend, but keep an eye on your values (remember, financial minimalism is about intentionality).

---

2. Embrace Frugality as a Lifestyle

Living below your means isn't about never spending money; it's about being strategic. Here are some strategies to embrace:

- **Meal Planning**: Cooking at home saves a ton compared to dining out. Plan meals for the week and create a grocery list to avoid impulse buys.

- **Buy Second-Hand**: Thrift shops and online marketplaces like Facebook Marketplace or Poshmark can be goldmines for quality items at a fraction of the cost.

- **Practice the 30-Day Rule**: Before making a non-essential purchase, wait 30 days. Often, you'll find the urge to buy fades, and if it doesn't, you can reassess.

Want to avoid overspending? Pretend every item in your online shopping cart is a subscription service that will charge you forever. Instant deterrent!

Your Day 5 Action Plan

1. **Audit and Cancel Unnecessary Subscriptions**: Use an app or go old-school with a highlighter and your bank statement.

2. **Negotiate Your Bills**: Make a list of bills you can try to lower and schedule time to make those calls.

3. **Simplify Your Bank Accounts**: Streamline your finances to only the accounts you really need.

4. **Adopt the Anti-Budget**: Set up automatic savings and live within your means—minimalism style.

By cutting financial clutter and unnecessary expenses, you're not just saving money—you're also saving time and mental energy.

Every step you take today brings you closer to financial freedom and a simpler, more intentional life.

Day 6: Building an Emergency Fund Quickly

If financial security were a fortress, your emergency fund would be the high, unbreakable walls guarding you from life's unexpected attacks. Emergencies don't send a "Save the Date"— they crash into your life uninvited and expensive. Day 6 is all about making sure you're prepared when that happens.

Why You Need an Emergency Fund Now

First things first: Why all the fuss about an emergency fund? Well, life can be unpredictable. Whether it's a medical emergency, a sudden job loss, or your car breaking down at the worst possible moment, having a financial cushion can mean the difference between a minor inconvenience and a life-altering crisis.

Financial Security in a Crisis

Without an emergency fund, even small emergencies can force you into debt, whether through credit cards or loans. The idea is to have at least three to six months' worth of living expenses set aside so you can weather life's storms without going under financially.

Example: Imagine your hot water heater explodes. Without an emergency fund, you'd have to use a high-interest credit card to pay for repairs, which could turn a $1,000 problem into a financial burden lasting months or years.

Accelerating Your Savings Strategy

Time is money, and we're going to save both. Here's how to build up your emergency fund faster, even if you're working with a tight budget.

1. Automate Your Savings

Automation makes saving effortless and consistent. Set up a direct deposit from your paycheck into a high-yield savings account. Even if you start small, the habit will grow over time.

Pro Tip: Use the "pay yourself first" strategy—allocate a percentage of your income to savings before paying bills or buying anything discretionary. Treat it like a mandatory expense.

2. Use Windfalls Wisely

Any unexpected money you receive, like tax refunds, work bonuses, or even birthday cash, should go straight into your emergency fund. It's tempting to splurge, but investing in your financial safety will bring you more long-term satisfaction.

Sure, you *could* blow that bonus on a shiny new gadget, or you could deposit it into your emergency fund and sleep better at night. Consider this your grown-up version of "choosing your adventure."

3. Slash Expenses and Redirect the Savings

Remember the financial clutter we tackled on Day 5? The money you freed up from canceling subscriptions or negotiating bills should now have a new home—your emergency fund. Here are some creative ways to accelerate this:

- **Go on a No-Spend Challenge**: Pick a week (or a whole month, if you're feeling brave) where you only spend on essentials. All the money you save goes into your fund.

- **Sell Unused Items**: Decluttering can be both therapeutic and profitable. Use online marketplaces like eBay, Poshmark, or Facebook Marketplace to sell clothes, gadgets, or furniture you no longer need.

Maintaining a Dedicated Safety Net

Building your emergency fund is a triumph, but maintaining it requires discipline. Here's how to make sure your hard-earned safety net stays intact.

1. Keep Your Fund Separate and Inaccessible

Your emergency fund should live in a separate, high-yield savings account. This keeps it out of sight and less tempting to spend while still earning some interest.

Why High-Yield Savings? Unlike regular savings accounts, high-yield accounts offer higher interest rates, so your money grows over time. It's not investment-level returns, but hey, free money is free money.

2. Define What "Emergency" Means

Before you dip into your fund, ask yourself if the expense genuinely qualifies as an emergency. Here's a handy guideline:

- **True Emergencies**: Job loss, medical expenses, urgent home or car repairs.

- **Not Emergencies**: Vacations, impulse purchases, or those shoes you've been eyeing on sale.

Mental Hack: Create a list of what you consider genuine emergencies and post it somewhere visible. This will serve as a reality check when you're tempted to withdraw money.

Your Day 6 Action Plan

1. **Automate Your Savings**: Set up a recurring transfer from your main account to your emergency fund. Start with whatever amount you can manage, and increase it over time.

2. **Redirect Windfalls**: Commit to depositing any extra money you receive directly into your fund.

3. **Challenge Yourself to Save**: Try a no-spend week or sell unused items to boost your savings.

4. **Open a High-Yield Savings Account**: If you don't have one already, research banks that offer competitive rates and minimal fees.

Building an emergency fund quickly isn't just a nice idea; it's a financial priority. Once you've established your safety net, you'll experience a new level of financial peace and confidence. Future-you will be eternally grateful.

Day 7: Effective Debt Elimination Techniques

You've made it to Day 7—congratulations! By now, you've learned how to simplify your finances and boost your emergency fund, so it's time to address one of the biggest barriers to financial peace: debt. Getting rid of debt can feel overwhelming, but with a clear plan and effective techniques, you can make steady progress toward becoming debt-free.

High-Impact Debt Repayment Methods (Snowball vs. Avalanche)

When it comes to debt repayment strategies, two popular approaches dominate: the Debt Snowball and the Debt Avalanche. Both are proven to work, but they have different philosophies.

1. The Debt Snowball Method

The Debt Snowball method is all about momentum. Here's how it works:

- List your debts from smallest to largest, regardless of the interest rate.

- Pay the minimums on all your debts except the smallest. Throw every extra dollar at the smallest debt until it's gone.

- Once you've paid off the smallest debt, roll that payment into the next smallest, and so on, like a snowball gathering size as it rolls downhill.

Pros: The psychological wins of paying off smaller debts quickly can keep you motivated. It's a great method if you need frequent encouragement to stay on track.

Cons: You may pay more in interest over time compared to other methods, especially if your larger debts have high interest rates.

2. The Debt Avalanche Method

The Debt Avalanche method is designed to save you the most money in interest payments. Here's how it works:

- List your debts from highest to lowest interest rate.

- Pay the minimums on all your debts, and focus all extra funds on the debt with the highest interest rate. Once that's paid off, move to the next highest, and so on.

Pros: You'll pay less interest overall, which means you become debt-free faster from a purely financial perspective.

Cons: It can take longer to see results, especially if your highest-interest debt has a large balance, which might make it harder to stay motivated.

Which Method Is Right for You? It comes down to your psychology and financial situation. If you need quick wins to stay motivated, go with the Snowball. If you're more numbers-driven and want to minimize interest costs, the Avalanche may be better.

Understanding When to Consolidate or Refinance

Debt consolidation and refinancing are tools that can simplify your repayment plan and potentially lower your interest rates. Here's a breakdown of when these strategies make sense.

1. Debt Consolidation

Debt consolidation involves combining multiple debts into one loan with a single monthly payment, often at a lower interest rate. This can be particularly helpful if you're juggling several high-interest credit cards.

When to Consider It:

- If the new loan has a lower interest rate than your current debts.

- If managing multiple payments is overwhelming.

- If you can get a loan with better repayment terms.

Caution: Be careful of consolidation loans with hidden fees or if you're tempted to rack up more debt after consolidating.

2. Refinancing

Refinancing is taking out a new loan to pay off existing debt, typically with better terms. People often refinance mortgages, car loans, or student loans to save on interest.

When to Consider It:

- If interest rates have dropped since you took out your original loan.

- If your credit score has improved, making you eligible for better rates.

- If you need to adjust your loan terms (e.g., extending your repayment period for lower monthly payments).

Pro Tip: Always shop around and read the fine print. Refinancing and consolidating should make your debt easier to manage, not add to your burden.

Staying Motivated on Your Debt-Free Journey

Debt repayment is a marathon, not a sprint. Staying motivated is key to reaching the finish line, so let's talk about ways to keep your momentum strong.

1. Track Your Progress Visually

Seeing your progress can be incredibly motivating. Consider creating a debt payoff chart or using a mobile app to track how much you've paid and how far you have to go.

Fun Idea: Create a "Debt Thermometer" that you fill in as you pay off more debt. Hang it somewhere visible to remind yourself of your progress.

2. Celebrate Milestones (Responsibly)

When you pay off a debt or reach a major milestone, reward yourself—but within reason. Choose something small and meaningful, like a celebratory dinner or a new book. The key is to celebrate without derailing your financial goals.

Just don't celebrate paying off a credit card by using that same card for a splurge. We're trying to get *out* of debt, not do a celebratory moonwalk back into it!

3. Remember Your "Why"

Stay connected to your reasons for becoming debt-free. Maybe it's to buy a home, save for your children's education, or simply sleep better at night. Write down your "why" and refer to it whenever you feel discouraged.

Reflective Exercise: Write a letter to your future self, describing what being debt-free will mean for you. Seal it up and open it when you're struggling to stay motivated.

Your Day 7 Action Plan

1. **Choose Your Debt Repayment Strategy**: Decide if the Debt Snowball or Avalanche method suits you best and map out your debts accordingly.

2. **Explore Consolidation and Refinancing Options**: Do some research and see if either option could save you money or simplify your repayment plan.

3. **Create a Motivation System**: Set up a visual tracker or a rewards system to keep your spirits high on your debt-free journey.

Eliminating debt is one of the most freeing and empowering things you can do for your financial future. Take it one step at a time, and remember: Every dollar you pay off brings you closer to freedom and a simpler, more intentional life.

Day 8: Developing Smart Spending Habits

Welcome to Day 8! Today, we're shifting gears from tackling debt to one of the most crucial aspects of financial minimalism: spending. This is where your daily financial decisions can make or break your long-term money goals. The aim isn't to never spend money—it's to spend wisely and in line with your values. Let's dive in!

The Art of Intentional Spending

Intentional spending is all about making conscious choices with your money, rather than letting habits or impulses drive your purchases. It's about aligning your spending with your values, goals, and overall financial plan.

1. Understand Your Values and Priorities

Before you spend, ask yourself: *Does this purchase align with my values?* Maybe you value health, in which case investing in a quality gym membership or fresh produce makes sense. If your priority is financial freedom, then splurging on a new gadget every month may not be the best choice.

Exercise: Write down your top three financial values and revisit them whenever you're faced with a spending decision. This way, you can evaluate whether a purchase contributes to or detracts from your priorities.

2. Create a 24-Hour Rule for Discretionary Spending

Impulse buying is the enemy of financial minimalism. Implement a 24-hour (or even 30-day) rule: wait before making any non-essential purchase. This buffer period gives you time to determine if you truly need or even want the item.

Example: See a stylish new jacket? Give it 24 hours. If you still want it after considering your budget and values, then you can revisit the decision. Often, the urge passes.

Think of impulse purchases as "financial junk food." Tasty in the moment, but you might regret it the next day when your wallet feels bloated.

Cash vs. Credit: Making the Right Choices

Both cash and credit have their place, but how and when you use each can significantly impact your financial health.

1. The Case for Cash

Paying with cash can be a powerful way to curb overspending. When you physically hand over cash, you feel the "pain" of parting with your money, making you less likely to spend recklessly.

Practical Tip: Try using the "cash envelope system" for discretionary expenses like dining out, groceries, or entertainment. Allocate a set amount of cash for each category. When the envelope is empty, you're done spending for the month.

2. The Strategic Use of Credit

Credit cards aren't all bad; they can be useful for building your credit score and earning rewards, but only if you use them wisely.

- **Never carry a balance**: Always pay off your card in full to avoid interest charges.

- **Use credit strategically**: Only use your card for planned purchases, and treat it like cash by immediately setting aside the money to pay it off.

Warning: Be wary of using credit cards for everyday expenses if you have trouble controlling spending. The convenience can quickly lead to overspending and, ultimately, debt.

Pro Tip: Consider automating your credit card payments so you never miss a due date, but regularly review your statements to catch any errors or fraudulent charges.

Maximizing Value Without Sacrificing Quality

One of the tenets of financial minimalism is spending less without compromising on what matters to you. This doesn't mean buying the cheapest option every time—it means getting the most value for your dollar.

1. Invest in Quality for High-Use Items

It might seem counterintuitive, but sometimes spending more upfront saves money in the long run. For items you use regularly, like shoes, a mattress, or a quality coat, investing in durable, high-quality options will cost less over time compared to replacing cheaper, poorly-made items.

Example: Instead of buying a cheap coffee maker that breaks in six months, invest in one that's built to last. You'll enjoy better coffee and avoid repeat spending.

2. Master the Art of Comparison Shopping

Thanks to technology, comparison shopping is easier than ever. Before making a major purchase, compare prices across multiple retailers and check for sales, coupons, or cashback offers.

Tools to Help You Save:

- **Honey**: A browser extension that automatically finds and applies coupon codes at checkout.

- **CamelCamelCamel**: A site that tracks the price history of Amazon products, so you know if you're getting a good deal.

- **Rakuten**: Earn cashback on purchases at participating retailers.

3. Buy Used or Borrow When Possible

Not everything needs to be bought new. For items like books, furniture, or even cars, buying used can save you a substantial amount without sacrificing quality.

Practical Exercise: Next time you need something, check local thrift stores, online marketplaces, or consider borrowing from a friend. For infrequent use items, like a power drill, borrowing or renting might be the best choice.

Think of it as adopting pre-loved items—like giving a second life to that barely-used yoga mat your neighbor swore she'd use every day.

Your Day 8 Action Plan

1. **Reflect on Your Spending Habits**: Write down three areas where you could be more intentional. Maybe it's eating out, entertainment, or online shopping.

2. **Test the Cash vs. Credit Approach**: Pick a spending category and use only cash for a month. Track how it affects your budget and spending habits.

3. **Commit to Comparison Shopping**: Before any significant purchase, take five minutes to compare prices or look for discounts. Make this a habit.

Today's goal is to empower you to make smarter, more thoughtful spending choices. By prioritizing value and aligning purchases with your values, you'll create a more meaningful and financially healthy life.

How are these habits resonating with you? Let me know if you'd like to dive deeper into any section or if you need more examples or practical tips!

Day 9: Simplified Investing for Beginners

Investing can seem like a complicated, jargon-filled world, but today we're going to strip it down to the basics. By the end of Day 9, you'll understand why investing is crucial, how to approach it simply, and ways to build a balanced portfolio without needing a finance degree.

Investing Fundamentals and Why They Matter

First, let's address the "why." Investing is your ticket to growing your wealth over time. Unlike saving, which preserves your wealth, investing has the power to multiply it. But remember, investing comes with risks, so understanding the basics is essential.

1. The Magic of Compound Interest

Albert Einstein famously called compound interest the "eighth wonder of the world." In simple terms, it's the process where your money earns returns, and then those returns earn even more returns. The earlier you start investing, the more time your money has to grow exponentially.

Example: If you invest $1,000 at an annual return of 7% (the average historical return of the stock market), it will double approximately every 10 years. By year 30, your $1,000 will grow to about $7,600 without you doing anything extra. That's the power of compound growth.

2. Risk vs. Reward

Every investment carries some level of risk, and typically, the higher the potential reward, the higher the risk. Understanding your risk tolerance (how much loss you can tolerate emotionally and financially) is a crucial first step.

Pro Tip: Your investment timeline also impacts your risk tolerance. If you're young and saving for retirement, you have more time to recover from market downturns, so you can afford more risk. If you're nearing retirement, a more conservative approach may be best.

Choosing Simple, Low-Risk Investment Strategies

Minimalist investing doesn't mean avoiding risk altogether; it means choosing investments that are straightforward, effective, and aligned with your goals. Here are a few beginner-friendly strategies:

1. Index Funds and ETFs (Exchange-Traded Funds)

Index funds and ETFs are popular choices for minimalist investors. Instead of trying to beat the market, they match the performance of a market index, like the S&P 500. They're low-cost, diversified, and don't require constant monitoring.

- **Why They Work**: They spread your risk across many companies, making them less volatile than individual stocks. Plus, the fees are much lower compared to actively managed funds.

- **Example**: Vanguard's Total Stock Market Index Fund is a common pick for beginner investors because it offers exposure to the entire U.S. stock market at a low cost.

Think of index funds like a buffet of stocks—you're not just betting on one dish (or company), but instead tasting a bit of everything to minimize disappointment.

2. Target-Date Funds

If you want a "set it and forget it" option, consider target-date funds. These funds automatically adjust your asset allocation (the mix of stocks and bonds) based on your age and retirement timeline.

- **How They Work**: You pick a fund with a target date close to when you plan to retire, and the fund gradually becomes more conservative as that date approaches.

Pros: Target-date funds take the guesswork out of investing, making them ideal for those who prefer minimal involvement.

Cons: They may not be as customizable as managing your investments separately, but for many people, the simplicity is worth it.

How to Balance Risk in a Minimalist Portfolio

Balancing risk is about diversifying your investments so that a downturn in one area doesn't derail your entire financial plan. A common minimalist strategy involves a mix of stocks, bonds, and perhaps some alternative investments.

1. Understanding Asset Allocation

Your asset allocation is the ratio of stocks to bonds in your portfolio. A simple rule of thumb: Subtract your age from 100 to determine the percentage you should allocate to stocks. If you're 30, that means 70% in stocks and 30% in bonds.

Example Portfolios:

- **Aggressive (young investors)**: 80% stocks, 20% bonds

- **Balanced (middle-aged investors)**: 60% stocks, 40% bonds

- **Conservative (near retirement)**: 40% stocks, 60% bonds

Note: These are just guidelines. Your personal risk tolerance and goals should dictate your specific allocation.

2. Diversification Made Simple

Diversification is a fancy term for not putting all your eggs in one basket. By spreading your investments across different asset classes (like U.S. stocks, international stocks, and bonds), you minimize the impact of any single investment performing poorly.

Minimalist Approach: A simple two- or three-fund portfolio using broad index funds can give you all the diversification you need. For example, a common setup is:

- U.S. Total Stock Market Index Fund

- International Stock Market Index Fund

- U.S. Total Bond Market Index Fund

Your Day 9 Action Plan

1. **Define Your Risk Tolerance**: Think about how you react to market volatility and determine if you're more comfortable with a higher or lower risk portfolio.

2. **Choose Your Investment Vehicles**: Decide if index funds, ETFs, or a target-date fund make sense for your goals.

3. **Open an Investment Account**: If you don't have one already, look into robo-advisors like Betterment or traditional platforms like Vanguard or Fidelity.

4. **Set Up Automatic Contributions**: Automating your investments ensures consistency and takes the emotion out of the process.

Investing may feel complex, but simplicity is often the best approach. By starting small and staying consistent, you'll set yourself on a path to long-term financial security. Remember, the earlier you start, the more you benefit from the magic of compounding.

Day 10: Automating Your Finances for Long-Term Success

Congratulations on reaching Day 10! At this point, you've done the hard work of understanding financial minimalism, setting goals, and building a solid foundation for wealth. Now, it's time to future-proof your finances by making the process as effortless as possible. Automation is the secret sauce that helps your money grow with minimal intervention. Today, we'll explore how to set up automatic systems that do the heavy lifting while ensuring you remain in control.

Benefits of Financial Automation

Automating your finances isn't just about convenience—it's a powerful strategy that reduces stress, eliminates the risk of missed payments, and ensures that you stick to your saving and investing plans.

1. Consistency Is Key

One of the biggest hurdles in personal finance is consistency. It's all too easy to forget to transfer money to your savings or investment account or to pay a bill on time. Automation removes this risk, making sure that your financial goals are prioritized before any "extra" spending tempts you.

Think of automation as your highly efficient, unpaid assistant who never calls in sick, takes coffee breaks, or has "off" days.

2. Time-Saving Superpower

Manually managing your money every month can be tedious. Automating recurring payments and transfers saves you time and reduces the cognitive load of making the same decisions repeatedly.

Pro Tip: Time is money, and by reclaiming hours spent juggling financial tasks, you can focus on more meaningful pursuits.

3. Building Wealth on Autopilot

Automation ensures that you're always investing in your future. Whether it's saving for retirement or growing an emergency fund, automated contributions mean your money is quietly working for you in the background. This not only accelerates your progress but also leverages the power of compound interest over time.

Setting Up Automatic Savings and Investment Plans

Ready to automate your way to financial success? Here's a step-by-step guide to automating your savings and investments:

1. Automate Your Savings First

Your financial foundation starts with savings, and it's essential to prioritize it. Set up automatic transfers from your checking account to your savings account on the day you receive your paycheck.

- **Emergency Fund**: If you're still building your emergency fund, automate a portion of your paycheck to go directly into this fund. This should be a high-priority task until you have at least 3-6 months' worth of expenses saved.

- **Goal-Specific Savings**: For other savings goals (like a vacation or a new car), consider opening separate savings accounts. Many banks allow you to create "buckets" within your savings account to organize your money for specific goals.

Example: If your paycheck hits on the 1st and 15th of every month, set up an automatic transfer to savings on those same days.

2. Automate Your Investment Contributions

Next, ensure that your investments are growing steadily. If you have a 401(k) or employer-sponsored retirement plan, contributions are often automated by default. But don't stop there—set up automatic contributions to your Individual Retirement Account (IRA) or brokerage account as well.

- **Retirement Accounts**: If possible, max out your 401(k) contributions or set a percentage of your income that feels manageable. The earlier you start, the more your money can grow.

- **Robo-Advisors**: If you're using a robo-advisor like Betterment or Wealthfront, you can automate regular deposits. These platforms handle the investing for you, rebalancing your portfolio as needed.

Pro Tip: Aim to automate contributions to align with your payday. This way, you treat investing as a "non-negotiable expense," and you won't miss money you never see in your checking account.

3. Automate Your Bill Payments

Avoid late fees and keep your credit score intact by automating your recurring bills, such as utilities, rent, and credit card payments. Most banks and service providers offer an auto-pay option.

- **Minimum Payments for Credit Cards**: At the very least, set up automatic payments for the minimum amount due to avoid interest and fees. However, paying off your balance in full is always the best strategy.

- **Variable Bills**: For bills that fluctuate, like your electricity or water bill, automate the average amount and set a reminder to review and adjust as needed.

How to Stay in Control While Letting Automation Work

While automation is a game-changer, it doesn't mean you should set everything up and forget about it forever. Staying engaged and aware of your finances ensures that automation works for you, not against you.

1. Regularly Review Your Finances

Even though things are automated, check in with your finances monthly or quarterly. Make sure your goals are on track, and adjust your contributions if you get a raise, pay off a debt, or experience a significant life change.

Tip: Schedule a "money date" with yourself or your partner to review your financial health. Pour a cup of coffee, put on some calming music, and enjoy seeing your progress.

2. Build in Some Flexibility

Life is unpredictable, so it's essential to leave room for unexpected expenses or opportunities. Having a cash cushion in your checking account helps ensure that automated payments don't overdraft your account.

Example: If your monthly bills total $2,000, keep a buffer of $500-$1,000 in your checking account just in case.

3. Keep Your Financial Information Secure

With automation comes the responsibility of keeping your information safe. Use strong, unique passwords for your financial accounts and enable two-factor authentication where possible.

Reminder: Automation isn't a "set it and forget it" system—it's more like "set it, monitor, and adjust." By staying engaged, you ensure that your finances continue to align with your evolving goals.

Your Day 10 Action Plan

1. **Automate Your Savings**: Log into your bank and set up automatic transfers to your emergency fund and any goal-specific savings accounts.

2. **Automate Your Investments**: If you haven't already, automate contributions to your retirement accounts and brokerage accounts.

3. **Automate Your Bills**: Sign up for auto-pay on all your recurring bills. Use a credit card for payments if you earn rewards, but make sure the card is paid off monthly.

4. **Set Reminders for Check-Ins**: Add calendar reminders to review your finances regularly and adjust as needed.

Today, you've learned how to automate your way to financial peace of mind. By taking these steps, you're freeing up mental space, reducing stress, and ensuring your money is working efficiently behind the scenes. Great job making it this far—your future self will thank you!

Feel free to ask if you'd like deeper explanations, practical examples, or suggestions for specific financial tools!

Day 11: Embracing a Minimalist Lifestyle for Financial Health

Welcome to Day 11! By now, you've learned the nuts and bolts of managing your finances minimally. Today, we're focusing on how embracing a minimalist lifestyle overall can supercharge your financial health and bring more peace into your life.

Decluttering Your Space and Mind to Save Money

Minimalism isn't just about managing your money; it's about creating a more intentional, clutter-free life that aligns with your values. When you declutter your space, you declutter your mind and reduce the temptation to spend.

1. The Cost of Clutter

You might be surprised to know how much clutter costs you—literally and figuratively. Think about it: more stuff requires more space, more maintenance, and often leads to more stress. If you're renting a storage unit, buying organization supplies, or even just stressing over messes, it's costing you.

- **Action Step**: Spend some time decluttering your home. Start small, like your closet or kitchen, and work your way up to bigger spaces. Use the "three-box method": one for things to keep, one for things to donate, and one for things to discard.

Minimalist Tip: As you go through each item, ask yourself, "Does this add real value to my life?" If the answer is no, let it go. Remember, every item you keep should "earn" its place.

2. Decluttering Your Digital Life

Digital clutter can be just as overwhelming. Unsubscribe from emails that tempt you to spend, clean up your phone and computer, and set a simple folder system to keep things organized.

Your email inbox shouldn't look like a hoarder's garage. Aim for Inbox Zero, or at least something closer to Inbox "Not-Giving-Me-Anxiety."

Free Activities That Enrich Your Life

Living minimally doesn't mean depriving yourself of joy. In fact, it encourages you to seek out enriching experiences that don't come with a price tag. Here are some ideas:

1. Reconnect with Nature

Spending time outdoors is one of the most cost-effective ways to boost your mood and health. Go for a hike, have a picnic, or simply walk through a local park. Nature therapy is free, and it's scientifically proven to lower stress and improve well-being.

Example: Instead of meeting friends for dinner at an expensive restaurant, suggest a group hike or a potluck picnic at a nearby park. The experience will be memorable and wallet-friendly.

2. Explore Community Events

Many cities offer free or low-cost events, from art walks to outdoor movies to yoga in the park. Check your local community calendar to find hidden gems that won't dent your budget.

- **Pro Tip**: Libraries often host free workshops, book clubs, and other activities. Bonus: Libraries also have movies, eBooks, and audiobooks for free.

3. Get Creative at Home

If you enjoy being at home, embrace activities that make your space a haven. Host game nights, cook a new recipe with friends, or have a DIY spa day.

There's something weirdly satisfying about pampering yourself with homemade facemasks while binge-watching documentaries on minimalism.

Finding Happiness Beyond Material Goods

True happiness often comes from connections, experiences, and personal growth rather than from things. Here's how to cultivate contentment that doesn't require spending.

1. Practice Gratitude Daily

When you focus on what you're grateful for, you stop longing for more. Take a moment each day to write down three things you appreciate. This simple habit can dramatically shift your perspective and reduce the urge to buy more.

- **Action Step**: Keep a gratitude journal by your bedside. Every night, jot down what made you smile or feel content that day.

2. Invest in Relationships, Not Things

Experiences with loved ones provide lasting joy. Prioritize family dinners, meetups with friends, and quality time with people you cherish. These moments create memories that last a lifetime.

Example: Instead of buying a new gadget or piece of clothing, use that money to plan a memorable experience, like a day trip or a cooking class with a friend.

3. Mindful Consumption

When you do spend, do it with intention. Before making a purchase, ask yourself if it aligns with your values and brings long-term happiness. Often, you'll realize that the rush of retail therapy isn't worth the financial hangover.

If you've ever bought an item that ended up gathering dust in your closet, you know the feeling of shopper's remorse. Mindful spending helps you avoid those "what-was-I-thinking" moments.

Your Day 11 Action Plan

1. **Declutter**: Pick one area of your home and spend 30 minutes decluttering. Consider selling high-value items and putting the money toward debt repayment or your savings goals.

2. **Plan Free Experiences**: Make a list of free activities you want to try in the next month. Whether it's visiting a museum on a free admission day or having a beach day, schedule them into your calendar.

3. **Journal**: Start your gratitude practice tonight. Reflect on the non-material things that bring you happiness and how you can prioritize them moving forward.

By embracing a minimalist lifestyle, you're not just improving your financial health—you're enhancing your quality of life. Minimalism is about curating a life filled with purpose, connection, and experiences that matter. Keep this momentum going!

Day 12: Establishing a Financial Check-In Routine

It's Day 12, and we're almost at the end of your 2-week crash course! Today is all about making financial upkeep a part of your lifestyle. It's not enough to set goals and hope for the best—consistent check-ins ensure you're on the right path and help you course-correct as needed. But don't worry; financial check-ins don't have to be tedious or stressful. With the right habits, it can become a simple and empowering routine.

Creating Regular Budget Review Habits

Just like maintaining good health requires regular exercise, keeping your finances in shape needs routine check-ups. Setting up a regular budget review helps you stay aware of your spending, savings, and overall financial health.

1. Frequency Matters

Decide how often you want to review your finances. A weekly check-in is ideal for staying on top of spending and ensuring bills are paid, while a monthly review gives a broader overview of your budget and goals.

- **Weekly Check-Ins**: These should be short and sweet. Spend about 15-30 minutes reviewing your recent transactions. Are you staying within your budget categories? Do you need to adjust anything for the upcoming week?

- **Monthly Reviews**: Dedicate more time at the end of each month to evaluate your overall progress. Look at your spending trends, adjust budget categories if necessary, and ensure your goals are still realistic.

Pro Tip: Schedule your budget reviews like a recurring appointment in your calendar. Treat it like a commitment to yourself, not something you can easily brush off.

2. Make It Enjoyable

Yes, it's possible to make budget reviews less painful and even... fun? Light a candle, put on some relaxing music, or have a favorite treat while you go through your finances. It's all about creating a positive association.

Think of it as a date with your money. Sure, your budget may not wine and dine you, but it'll set you up for a comfortable future—if that's not commitment, what is?

Adjusting Goals as Circumstances Change

Life is unpredictable, and your financial goals should be flexible enough to adapt to those changes. Whether it's a sudden job loss, an unexpected medical expense, or a windfall of cash, being adaptable is key.

1. Re-Evaluate Short and Long-Term Goals

Review your goals regularly to ensure they still make sense. For example, if your income increases, you might decide to pay off debt faster or increase your investment contributions. If your expenses go up, you may need to pull back on non-essential spending.

- **Emergency Adjustments**: If a crisis hits, focus on maintaining stability. This might mean pausing investments or reducing debt payments temporarily to keep your cash flow healthy.

- **Windfall Strategy**: On the flip side, if you come into extra money, like a bonus or tax refund, have a plan to use it wisely. You could boost your emergency fund, pay down debt, or make an extra investment contribution.

Practical Example: Let's say you're saving for a vacation, but then your car breaks down and requires major repairs. You can temporarily redirect your vacation savings to cover the cost. Once your finances recover, you can resume saving for the fun stuff.

Monitoring Investments Without Getting Overwhelmed

Investing is crucial for long-term wealth building, but keeping track of your portfolio doesn't have to be a daily obsession. Here's how to monitor your investments efficiently:

1. Keep It Simple

Check your investments quarterly, unless you're actively buying or selling. This is often enough to see how your portfolio is performing and make adjustments if necessary.

- **Avoid Daily Checking**: Watching your investments every day can lead to unnecessary stress and impulsive decisions. Remember, investing is a long game. Stay focused on your strategy and resist the urge to react to every market swing.

Unless you're Warren Buffett, you don't need to check your portfolio every time the stock market sneezes.

2. Use Tools to Simplify Tracking

There are numerous apps and platforms designed to help you keep an eye on your investments without needing a finance degree. Use a portfolio tracker or an investment app to get a bird's-eye view of your assets.

- **Automated Alerts**: Many tools can send you alerts if there's a significant change in your investments, so you only have to pay attention when it really matters.

3. Understand When to Rebalance

Rebalancing is the process of adjusting your portfolio to maintain your desired asset allocation. If stocks have performed well and now make up a larger portion of your portfolio than you're comfortable with, you may need to rebalance.

- **Annual Review**: Once a year, review your asset allocation and make any necessary adjustments. This keeps your portfolio aligned with your risk tolerance and investment goals.

Your Day 12 Action Plan

1. **Set Up Your Check-In Schedule**: Decide on a frequency for your financial reviews. Add these appointments to your calendar, and stick to them.

2. **Do a Quick Budget Review**: Take 15 minutes to look over your budget today and see where you stand.

3. **Reflect on Your Goals**: Are they still relevant? Make any necessary adjustments and keep a record of your new plans.

4. **Check Your Investment Plan**: If you haven't looked at your investments in a while, do a quick review. Make

sure you're comfortable with your asset allocation and note any needed changes for your annual rebalance.

With a strong check-in routine, you're setting yourself up for long-term financial success. By keeping things simple and consistent, you'll stay on top of your finances without feeling overwhelmed. One more day to go in this crash course—let's make it count!

Day 13: Planning for the Future with Minimalist Principles

Congratulations on reaching Day 13! You've learned how to declutter your financial life, budget like a minimalist, and start investing without unnecessary stress. Today, we'll zoom out and consider your long-term financial future—because building wealth intentionally means thinking about what comes next.

Long-Term Wealth Planning

Minimalist wealth planning isn't about amassing as much as possible but rather aligning your future financial security with your values. It's about creating a life where financial freedom enables you to do what you love most, whether that means traveling the world, pursuing passion projects, or leaving a meaningful legacy.

1. Define Your Version of "Enough"

One core principle of minimalism is understanding what "enough" looks like for you. How much money do you need to feel secure and fulfilled? Answering this question will help you set realistic, personalized financial goals.

- **How to Calculate Your Financial Independence Number**: This number represents the amount of savings and investments you need to live comfortably without working. As a rough guideline, multiply your annual expenses by 25. This calculation, based on the 4% rule, gives you an idea of the investment portfolio required for early or traditional retirement.

- **Practical Example**: If your annual expenses are $40,000, you'd need roughly $1,000,000 invested to cover your needs sustainably.

"Enough" isn't about affording your pet dolphin's organic fish diet. Keep it realistic, unless you're planning to live the life of a billionaire philanthropist.

2. Diversifying and Simplifying Investments

While investing is crucial, you don't have to be a financial wizard to create a solid portfolio. Minimalist investing principles favor diversification with low-maintenance options.

- **Index Funds and ETFs**: Consider simple investment vehicles like index funds, which track the market with low fees and minimal hassle. These are great for long-term growth and require little hands-on management.

- **Set It and Forget It**: Automate contributions to your retirement accounts, such as a 401(k) or IRA, so you never miss a beat.

Pro Tip: Revisit your investment strategy once a year to ensure it still aligns with your goals and risk tolerance. It's a lot less stressful than checking the stock market every day.

Legacy and Estate Planning Simplified

Even if estate planning sounds like something for the ultra-wealthy, it's relevant to everyone. Simplifying your plans makes things easier for your loved ones and ensures your assets go where you want.

1. Essentials of Estate Planning

Estate planning includes creating a will, naming beneficiaries, and possibly setting up a trust. It's about more than passing on money—it's about providing clear instructions so your family doesn't face unnecessary stress.

- **Draft a Will**: Your will specifies how you want your assets distributed. It doesn't have to be complicated or costly; many online tools and templates are available.

- **Beneficiary Designations**: Ensure all your accounts (like retirement and investment accounts) have designated beneficiaries. This can often bypass the need for probate, making things simpler and faster for your heirs.

A will is like a love letter to your loved ones—but with fewer sonnets and more "Don't forget to feed the cat."

2. Simplifying Documents for Your Family

Compile a minimalist "Legacy Binder" containing important documents like your will, insurance policies, account passwords, and healthcare directives. Make it easy for your loved ones to manage your affairs.

- **Digital Estate Plan**: As part of your estate planning, don't forget your digital assets. Document how you'd like your online accounts handled.

Keeping Your Plans Flexible and Adaptable

Life throws curveballs, and a good financial plan has room to adapt. Minimalist planning is about staying prepared for changes while avoiding overcomplication.

1. Embracing Change Gracefully

Expect the unexpected—whether it's an economic downturn or a sudden job opportunity. Review your financial plans regularly to ensure they reflect your current life situation and goals.

- **Review Insurance Needs**: As your life changes, your insurance needs may, too. Make sure your coverage aligns with your current circumstances.

- **Emergency Fund Updates**: As you build wealth, consider whether your emergency fund should grow. For example, if you own more assets or start a family, you might need a larger cushion.

2. Goals Are Guidelines, Not Set in Stone

Don't be afraid to adjust your plans if they no longer fit. Minimalism teaches us that clinging too tightly to outdated goals can be as unhelpful as holding onto unused possessions.

Practical Tip: Once a year, take a moment to reflect on your long-term goals. Are you still passionate about them? Are there new opportunities you'd like to pursue? Keep the vision of your future fluid but focused.

Your Day 13 Action Plan

1. **Calculate Your Financial Independence Number**: Use the 4% rule or another retirement calculator to see how much you need for long-term security. This can provide a goal to work toward.

2. **Update or Create Your Will**: If you haven't made a will, now is the time. If you already have one, review it and make any necessary updates.

3. **Simplify Your Investment Strategy**: Check your portfolio to see if you can simplify and reduce fees. If it's too complicated, consider shifting to a simpler strategy like index fund investing.

4. **Set Up a Legacy Binder**: Collect all your essential documents and let a trusted family member know where to find them.

5. **Reflect and Adjust**: Take time to review your long-term goals. Have your priorities changed? Do you need to adjust your timeline or strategies?

Minimalist financial planning is about setting yourself up for a life of freedom and purpose. By staying flexible and intentional, you're ensuring a secure, happy future for yourself and your loved ones.

Day 14: Maintaining Motivation and Financial Minimalism

Congratulations! You've reached the last day of this crash course in minimalist money management. But remember, this isn't a finish line; it's the start of a lifelong journey. Day 14 is all about sustaining the habits you've worked so hard to develop and staying motivated to continue your minimalist financial lifestyle.

Success Stories and Real-Life Applications

Hearing about how others have successfully adopted minimalist financial principles can be incredibly inspiring. Here are some real-world applications to motivate you and demonstrate that it's possible to thrive on this path.

1. From Debt Overload to Financial Freedom

Many people have transformed their lives by simplifying their finances. Take, for example, individuals who have paid off tens of thousands of dollars in debt by prioritizing their goals, cutting out excess, and staying disciplined. Their secret? Consistency and clarity of purpose.

- **The Journey**: These success stories usually begin with a moment of reckoning—seeing the debt number and realizing that change is non-negotiable. By creating a minimalist budget, slashing unnecessary expenses, and employing debt payoff strategies like the snowball method, they became debt-free much sooner than they ever imagined.

"Imagine the sheer joy of finally cutting up a credit card. It's like a graduation ceremony but with scissors instead of a diploma."

2. The Joy of Less Stuff, More Security

Others have found immense satisfaction in scaling back their lifestyles to enjoy greater financial peace. These people sold homes, downsized belongings, and refocused on experiences rather than possessions.

- **Example**: One family sold their large house, moved into a smaller home, and used the profits to build an emergency fund and increase their retirement contributions. The outcome? More time, more money, and less stress.

79

Tips for Avoiding Lifestyle Inflation

It's easy to fall into the trap of lifestyle inflation—spending more as you earn more. Here's how to avoid it and keep your finances in check:

1. Practice Gratitude

A key to maintaining minimalist living is contentment. Regularly practice gratitude for what you already have. When you focus on appreciating life's simple pleasures, the desire for material things tends to diminish.

Practical Tip: Keep a gratitude journal. Each day, write down one thing you're thankful for that doesn't involve spending money. It could be a beautiful sunset, a chat with a friend, or a moment of peace.

2. Set Clear Boundaries for Spending Increases

As your income grows, decide in advance how you'll allocate those extra dollars. Will 50% go to investments, 30% to your emergency fund, and 20% to treat yourself? By pre-assigning future income, you reduce the temptation to splurge mindlessly.

- **Example**: If you get a raise, consider automating higher contributions to your retirement fund or making an extra mortgage payment before you're tempted to increase your lifestyle.

"Remember, a bigger paycheck doesn't mean you need a bigger avocado toast budget. Or does it?"

3. Embrace "Enough"

Understand that more is not always better. Stick to your principles and avoid comparing your lifestyle to others. Remind yourself of your long-term goals, whether that's financial independence, early retirement, or having the freedom to pursue your dreams.

Your Path Forward: Continuous Minimalist Growth

Minimalism is a journey of continuous improvement. Here's how to keep evolving:

1. Set Yearly Challenges

Challenge yourself every year to declutter a new area of your financial life or adopt a new habit. This could be cutting another recurring expense, increasing your savings rate, or committing to a no-spend month.

- **Example**: You might decide to live on 80% of your income and invest the rest or see how long you can go without buying new clothes.

2. Keep Learning

Stay curious and engaged with financial education. Read books on personal finance, listen to podcasts, or join minimalist and financial independence communities. This keeps you motivated and introduces you to new strategies and ideas.

- **Recommended Reading**: Check out books like *Your Money or Your Life* by Vicki Robin or *The Simple Path to Wealth* by JL Collins.

3. Surround Yourself with Like-Minded People

The people you spend time with can greatly influence your habits. Seek out friends or groups that support your minimalist and financial goals. If you can't find them in person, connect with communities online.

"Find friends who think thrift stores are treasure hunts and budgeting apps are as exciting as dating apps. You'll be in good company."

Your Day 14 Action Plan

1. **Reflect on Your Journey**: Take a moment to think about how far you've come in these two weeks. Write down your biggest takeaways and any surprising lessons you've learned.

2. **Identify Your Next Financial Challenge**: Choose one area to work on next. It could be saving a certain amount in the next three months or cutting one more non-essential expense.

3. **Plan for Growth**: Make a plan to keep learning about minimalist money management. Schedule a monthly reminder to check in with your goals and celebrate your progress.

4. **Celebrate Your Success**: You've made it through 14 days of transformation! Reward yourself in a meaningful, non-material way, like a hike, a day spent doing something you love, or simply enjoying a quiet afternoon with a good book.

You've laid a strong foundation, but remember: the goal is progress, not perfection. Keep simplifying, keep growing, and keep living intentionally. Here's to a lifetime of financial peace and minimalist abundance!

Final Words

As we come to the end of our 2-Week Crash Course :,take a moment to celebrate your journey. These past two weeks have been a crash course not just in managing your money, but in rethinking your relationship with it. You've explored what it means to live intentionally, how to find joy in simplicity, and the immense power of prioritizing what truly matters.

Reflect on Your Progress

Remember, building wealth and living with purpose is not about sudden, monumental change but about the accumulation of small, thoughtful choices. The minimalist approach is your permission slip to step off the treadmill of consumerism and instead design a life aligned with your deepest values. You've decluttered not just your expenses but your mindset, finding freedom in knowing that every dollar has a job that brings you closer to your dreams.

Keep the Flame Alive

This journey doesn't end here. As you move forward, revisit your financial goals regularly and refine them as your life evolves. Stay curious, keep learning, and continue simplifying. Be kind to yourself when setbacks happen—they're just opportunities to grow.

Above all, remember that wealth is about more than just money. It's about the richness of experiences, the quality of your relationships, and the peace of mind that comes from knowing you're prepared for whatever comes your way. By living intentionally and practicing financial minimalism, you're giving yourself the gift of freedom—freedom from financial stress and freedom to live life on your terms.

A Note of Gratitude

Thank you for investing your time in this book and for trusting it as your guide. Your commitment to financial minimalism is a testament to your desire for a more intentional, fulfilling life. Go forward confidently, simplify where you can, and always choose what adds value over what adds clutter.

Here's to a future where you're not just wealthy in assets but also rich in the things that money can't buy. Keep striving, keep simplifying, and enjoy the wealth of possibilities that lie ahead!

Glossary

Assets

Anything of value owned by an individual or business, such as cash, stocks, real estate, or equipment.

Budget

A plan that outlines expected income and expenses over a set period, helping individuals manage their money more effectively.

Cash Flow

The movement of money in and out of an individual's account, encompassing income, expenses, and savings.

Compound Interest

Interest calculated on the initial principal and on any accumulated interest from previous periods, allowing savings or investments to grow faster over time.

Credit Score

A number representing an individual's creditworthiness, used by lenders to assess the risk of lending money.

Debt-to-Income Ratio (DTI)

A measure comparing an individual's monthly debt payments to their gross monthly income, used to assess financial stability.

Discretionary Spending

Money spent on non-essential items or services, such as entertainment or dining out.

Diversification

A strategy of spreading investments across various assets to reduce risk.

Emergency Fund

A savings reserve set aside to cover unexpected expenses, such as medical bills, car repairs, or job loss.

Equity

The value of ownership in an asset, such as the portion of a home owned outright without loans.

Expense Ratio

A measure of the cost to manage an investment fund, expressed as a percentage of the fund's assets.

Financial Freedom

The state of having sufficient savings and investments to afford one's lifestyle without relying on a traditional job.

Fixed Expenses

Regular, consistent costs that do not vary much month-to-month, such as rent, mortgage payments, and insurance.

Frugality

A lifestyle choice focused on reducing unnecessary spending and maximizing savings.

Income

Money earned through employment, investments, or other sources, contributing to an individual's cash flow.

Inflation

The general increase in prices over time, reducing the purchasing power of money.

Interest

The cost of borrowing money, or the return earned on an investment, typically expressed as a percentage.

Liabilities

Any financial obligations or debts an individual or business owes, such as loans or credit card debt.

Liquidity

The ease with which an asset can be quickly converted into cash without a significant loss in value.

Minimalism

A lifestyle philosophy focused on simplicity, reducing clutter, and emphasizing essential needs over excess.

Net Worth

The total value of an individual's assets minus liabilities, representing their overall financial standing.

Opportunity Cost

The potential gain lost when choosing one alternative over another, often used to evaluate financial decisions.

Passive Income

Income earned with little to no active effort, such as rental income, dividends, or royalties.

Pay Yourself First

A strategy of prioritizing savings by setting aside a portion of income before covering expenses.

Principal

The initial amount of money invested or borrowed, excluding interest or earnings.

Recession

A period of economic decline, typically marked by reduced spending, high unemployment, and shrinking GDP.

Return on Investment (ROI)

A measure of the profitability of an investment, calculated as a percentage of the initial investment cost.

Risk Tolerance

An individual's comfort level with the potential for loss in their investments.

Sinking Fund

A fund set up to save gradually for a specific, often large, future expense, like a vacation or a major purchase.

Variable Expenses

Costs that fluctuate month-to-month, such as utilities, groceries, and entertainment.

About the Author

Maxwell W. Wilson is a passionate lifelong learner with a background in Information Technology and Contemporary Marketing. He believes that knowledge should be both enlightening and enjoyable—a philosophy he brings into every book he writes. For Maxwell, writing is more than just sharing information; it's about creating a journey where readers engage, learn, and have fun. His commitment to rigorous research ensures that every detail is spot-on, while his lively writing style keeps readers captivated. Whether you're diving into new concepts or brushing up on the familiar, Maxwell's books promise an experience that's both informative and refreshingly entertaining.

For a behind-the-scenes look at Maxwell's latest thoughts and projects, you can find him on Instagram under the handle @anotsowiseoldman.

www.ingramcontent.com/pod-product-compliance
Lightning Source LLC
Chambersburg PA
CBHW052331220526
45472CB00001B/376